HANUKKAH FUN

KINGFISHER
BOSTON

For Scott and Gemma,
Scarlet and Harriet

I hope that every Hanukkah is packed
full of fun for you all—J.B.

KINGFISHER
a Houghton Mifflin Company imprint
222 Berkeley Street
Boston, Massachusetts 02116
www.houghtonmifflinbooks.com

First published in 1996
2 4 6 8 10 9 7 5 3 1
1TR/0403/SF/FR/140MA

LIBRARY OF CONGRESS CATALOGING-IN-PUBLICATION DATA
Bastyra, Judy.
Hanukkah fun/Judy Bastyra, Catherine Ward.
—1st American ed.
p. cm.
Summary: A brief history of Hanukkah accompanies recipes, craft
projects, and other activities to help celebrate this holiday.
1. Hanukkah—Juvenile literature. 2. Jewish crafts—Juvenile literature.
[1. Hanukkah. 2. Hanukkah cookery. 3. Handicrafts.]
I. Ward, Catherine, ill. II. Title
BM729. H35B37 1996
296.4'35 dc20 96-15581 CIP AC

Editor: Emily Kent
Craft consultant: Katie Gayle

ISBN 0-7534-5684-2

Printed in China

CONTENTS

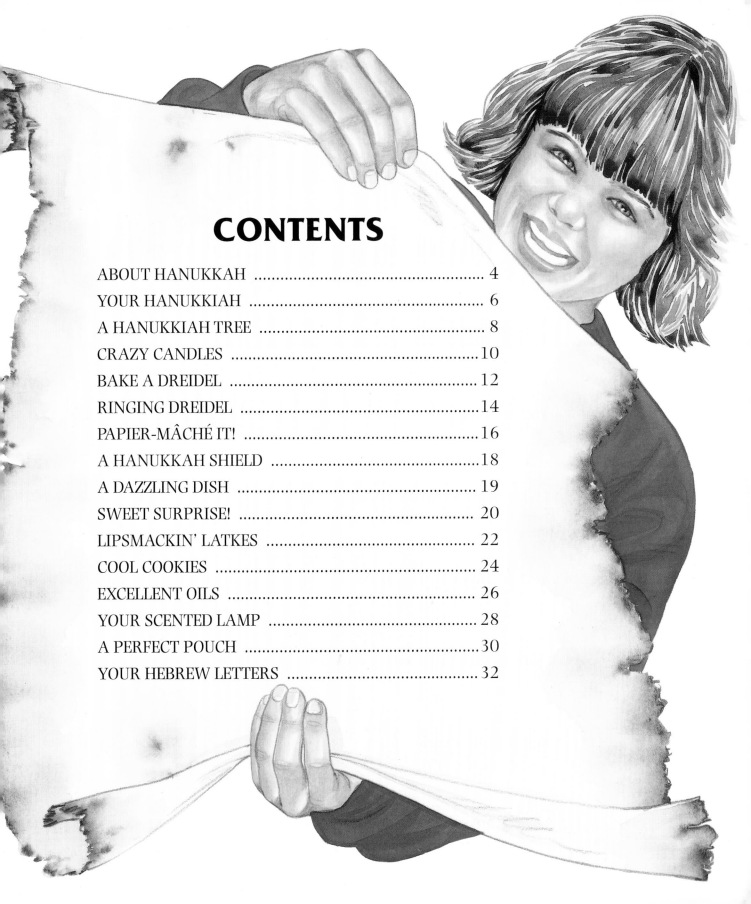

ABOUT HANUKKAH

Hanukkah is a festival of light and giving. It is celebrated by Jewish people all over the world. For eight days and nights candles are lit, and gifts are exchanged to celebrate a miracle that happened a long time ago in Judea—the land we now call Israel.

THE STORY OF HANUKKAH

More than 2,000 years ago the land of Judea was ruled by the Syrian king, Antiochus. He commanded that all the Jews in his kingdom were no longer to worship just one god but instead must convert to the Greek religion and worship many gods. Antiochus filled the holy temple in Jerusalem (the capital city of Judea) with idols and statues, and ordered the Jewish people to worship them.

If anyone disobeyed, Antiochus commanded his troops to set fire to their towns and villages and even to kill them! In the town of Modi'in lived Mattathias, a priest who led the Jewish resistance against Antiochus.

Mattathias fled with his family to live in the hills. Other Jewish families followed and a community was settled. Mattathias chose his son Judah Maccabee to lead this community. Judah formed a small army known as the Maccabees who were trained to surprise the Syrian army at night. After three long years, they won their battle and set about restoring the holy temple in Jerusalem. A special menorah was made for the temple, and enough oil was found to light the menorah for one day. But to everyone's amazement, the oil kept on burning—for eight days and nights! The miracle of Hanukkah was born . . . .

YOUR HANUKKIAH

A hanukkiah is a menorah used especially at Hanukkah. It holds nine candles and is the center of all the celebrations during this time. Each night, for eight nights, another candle is lit from one special candle—the Shamash, which means "helper." By the eighth day, all the candles have been lit. Try making your own hanukkiah, using clay, paint, and glue. Remember to make sure that the paint and glue you buy is safe to burn, and ask an adult to help with gluing and varnishing.

You will need

small pack (1lb) of DAS clay, gold acrylic paint, blunt knife, 9 candles, clear varnish, rolling pin and board, paint brushes, old newspaper or sheets of plastic

SIMPLE HANUKKIAH

1 Organize your work surface by covering a table with sheets of old newspaper or plastic.

2 Divide the clay into four equal lumps.

3 Roll out each lump into a long tube shape.

4 Twist two clay tubes to make a loose chain. Add a candle to each twist until you have put in nine candles. Twist the other two clay tubes over the first two for the second layer.

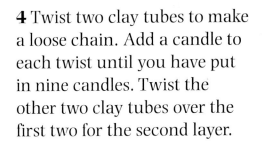

5 Gently press the two layers together and trim off the extra clay.

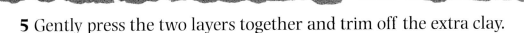

6 Roll your trimmings into another, shorter, tube and wind this gently around the first candle only. This makes a third layer for the Shamash—the candle you use to light all the other candles.

7 Place your hanukkiah in a warm place to dry out for a couple of days. Now you're ready to take out the candles and paint the hanukkiah gold. When the paint is dry, ask an adult to help you put a coat of varnish on it. Leave it to dry completely before you light the first candle for Hanukkah.

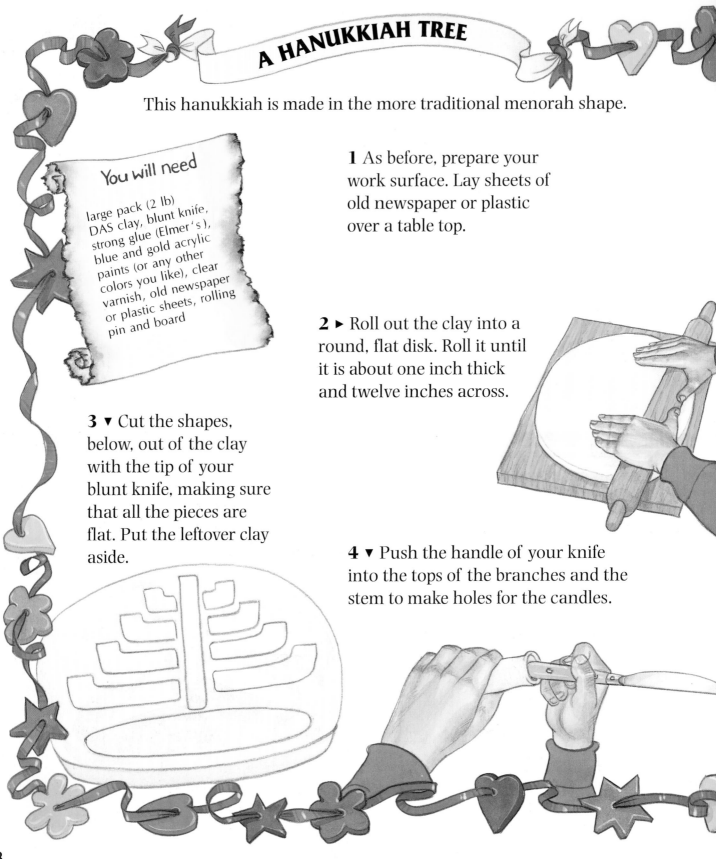

A HANUKKIAH TREE

This hanukkiah is made in the more traditional menorah shape.

You will need

large pack (2 lb) DAS clay, blunt knife, strong glue (Elmer's), blue and gold acrylic paints (or any other colors you like), clear varnish, old newspaper or plastic sheets, rolling pin and board

1 As before, prepare your work surface. Lay sheets of old newspaper or plastic over a table top.

2 ► Roll out the clay into a round, flat disk. Roll it until it is about one inch thick and twelve inches across.

3 ▼ Cut the shapes, below, out of the clay with the tip of your blunt knife, making sure that all the pieces are flat. Put the leftover clay aside.

4 ▼ Push the handle of your knife into the tops of the branches and the stem to make holes for the candles.

5 ▶ Leave the pieces of your tree to dry in a warm place for at least two days. Keep turning them over—gently—until they are completely dry. Then glue all the connecting pieces together—very carefully—until you have a complete "tree."

7 ▶ Now lay your hanukkiah down on old newspaper and leave it so that the glue can dry. Once the glue has set firm, you can start painting—how about deep blue, or bright pink?

8 ▼ Make small decorative shapes with leftover clay. When they are dry, paint them, let the paint dry, and glue them onto your hanukkiah. Finally, ask an adult to cover your hanukkiah with a coat of varnish. . .magnificent!

CRAZY CANDLES

It's simple and fun decorating candles for a hanukkiah, or for around your home. Make sure you *always* ask an adult to light the candles, and check carefully that your paints and glue are safe to burn. Crayons, acrylic paint, and glitter are usually safe.

CRAYON CANDLES

An easy way to decorate your candles is to use melted crayons.

1 Put a plain candle in the candle holder and ask an adult to light it.

2 Keeping your fingers out of reach of the flame, hold a crayon over the candle, and let it drip onto the candle below.

You will need

colored crayons
plain white candles
a candle holder

You can make patterns using different colored crayons—dots, stripes, and so on. See how many different patterns you can make!

It's hard finding things that will stick to the slippery surface of the candles, but acrylic paint does and is very easy to use. Here are some ideas for decorating your candles using acrylic paints.

You will need

acrylic paints
paint brushes
an old plate
a candle holder
glitter, sequins

1 Stand the candles in a hanukkiah, or candle holder, so you don't get messy hands!

2 Using your paints, paint whatever design you like on your candle.

SPARKLING CANDLES

1 ▼ Pour some glitter onto a plate. Paint a candle, and roll it in the glitter.

2 ▼ Add sequins to your glitter for extra sparkle!

3 For textured candles, make a mix of paint and glitter. Roll your candle in the mixture!

BAKE A DREIDEL

This salt-dough dreidel looks stunning as a table or mantel decoration . . . .

You will need

1 cup of flour, half cup of salt, tablespoon of cooking oil, half cup of water, plastic bag, baking sheet, white glue, clear acrylic varnish, glitter glue in bright colors, felt-tip pen

SALT DOUGH

Mix the flour, salt, oil, and water together in a bowl until a dough is formed. Knead the dough on a work surface for a few minutes until it is smooth. Place the salt dough in a plastic bag to keep it from drying out until you're ready to use it.

MAKING THE DREIDEL

1 ▸ Ask an adult to preheat the oven to 200°F. Roll the salt dough into a tube shape, about two inches across.

2 ▸ Form into a cube by pressing each side onto the work surface. Then pull the dough out at one end to make a handle.

3 ▸ Form the other end of the cube into a point. Place on a baking sheet, and ask an adult to put it in the oven for two hours.

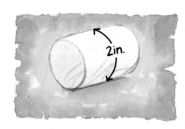

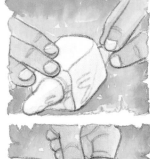

4 ▾ When it is baked dry and has completely cooled, ask an adult to help paint it with a coat of varnish. Leave it to dry, resting it over an old mug or glass.

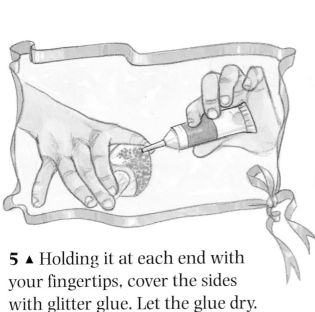

5 ▲ Holding it at each end with your fingertips, cover the sides with glitter glue. Let the glue dry.

6 ▲ Hold it by the middle. Cover the point and the handle with glitter glue.

נ כ ה ש

7 ▲ When the dreidel is dry, write Hebrew letters with a felt-tip pen on the sides, in the order shown above. (To find out what these letters mean, turn to page 96). Go over them with colored glitter glue. Wait for each letter to dry before going on to the next one.

8 Finally, ask an adult to cover the dreidel with a coat of varnish. Leave it to dry.

RINGING DREIDEL

This felt dreidel makes a great toy for a brother or sister—or you can use it to play the dreidel game on the next page.

You will need

a sheet of medium thick card-board, paper, felt-tip pens, blunt scissors, ruler, toy bell, wooden chopstick (painted gold), fabric glue, different colored felt, craft paper

1 ▾ Using the measurements shown, copy this shape onto cardboard and cut it out. Fold along the dotted lines, and glue down all the flaps except the top one.

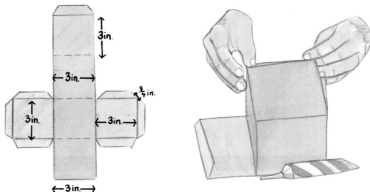

3in.

←3in.→

¾ in.

3in.

←3in.→

3in.

←3in.→

2 ▾ Put your bell inside, through the top of the cube, and glue down the top flap.

3 Cut out six three-inch felt squares in different colors. Glue a square onto each side of the cube. Make a hole at each end and push the chopstick through. Seal in place with a dab of glue.

4 Trace onto paper and cut out the four Hebrew letters on page 96. These will be your patterns. Tape them to felt, and cut out the felt letters. Glue the felt letters onto the sides of your cube.

Now you're ready to play Spin the Dreidel. You need between two and eight friends, sitting in a circle. Give each player an equal number of candies, fruit, nuts, or coins. Place a plate in the middle. Use your felt dreidel to play. Here is what the Hebrew letters mean in this game:

Nun means take nothing from the plate.
Gimel means take all.
Heh means take half.
Shin means put something on the plate.

SPIN THE DREIDEL

Each player puts the same amount of candies, nuts, etc., onto the plate, and spins the dreidel once. When it stops, the letter on top tells the player what to do.

The winner is the one who has the biggest pile when the plate is empty!

PAPIER-MÂCHÉ IT!

With this quick method you can create all kinds of wonderful things from papier-mâché.

PAPER PULP

Paper pulp can be stored for several weeks—and it is very simple to make.

You will need

old newspaper, hot water, an old plastic bowl, an airtight plastic container with a lid, rubber gloves

Wearing rubber gloves, tear the newspaper into strips into the plastic bowl. Cover the paper with plenty of hot water and let it soak—stir the mixture occasionally. When the paper is mushy, scoop it out of the bowl and squeeze out any extra water. Store the pulp in a plastic container, ready to use.

PAPIER-MÂCHÉ HELMET

You will need

a balloon, permanent felt-tip pen, two paintbrushes, Elmer's glue, paper pulp, blunt scissors, corrugated or plain cardboard, strips of newspaper, gold and silver acrylic paints, tissue paper

1 Blow up a balloon to a size slightly larger than your head.

2 ▶ Gently draw the outline of a helmet on it with a felt-tip pen.

3 Use one brush to apply a little glue inside the outline. Stick down newspaper strips until the helmet shape is covered.

4 Gently spread glue over the newspaper. Apply a thick layer of paper pulp over the top, patting it on gently. Leave it to dry for two days.

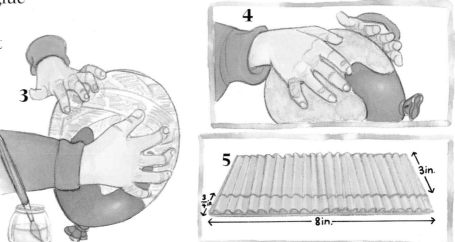

5 Cut a strip of cardboard (3 x 8 in.) and make a $^3/_4$-inch fold along one side for the base, as shown above.

6 Make deep cuts with your scissors from the top to the fold line, spaced $^3/_4$ inch apart. Then make cuts spaced $1^3/_4$ inches apart along the base up to the fold line.

7 Fold the bottom flaps to alternate sides. Once the helmet is dry, glue on the base flaps. Cut the tops into points, as below.

8 Glue a layer of tissue paper to the helmet and let it dry. Burst the balloon inside and cut off any hanging shreds. Paint the helmet silver and the "feathers" gold.

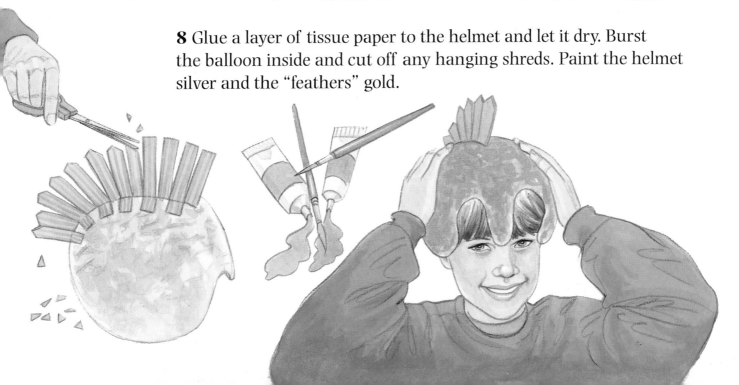

A HANUKKAH SHIELD

This shield will look great hanging on your bedroom wall.

← 12 in. →

45 in.

1 ▶ Copy this shield onto cardboard, to the measurements given. Ask an adult to help you cut it out and cover each side with a coat of varnish.

2 ▶ Cover the shield with paper pulp (see page 16), applying glue in small areas as you go. Let the shield dry for two days.

4 Paint on a Hebrew letter, a Star of David, or a dove of peace.

3 ▲ Make two holes at the top of the shield. Thread string through each hole and knot one end. Pull the string so the shield curves slightly. Knot the other end. Paint the shield a bright color and let it dry.

A DAZZLING DISH

This papier-mâché bowl makes a great candy dish, or a place to keep jewelry.

You will need

a small bowl for a mold, paper pulp, tissue paper, plastic wrap, gluestick, paper varnish, gold or silver acrylic paint, sequins or tiny beads

1 ▼ Cover the inside of your bowl with plastic wrap. Put glue over it.

2 ▼ Pat paper pulp over the glue, up to the rim, until you have an even layer.

3 ▶ Set the bowl aside until the pulp is firm enough to gently peel away the plastic wrap. Let it dry for 24 hours.

5 ▼ Paint your bowl silver or gold. When it's dry, glue on sequins or tiny beads. Varnish again.

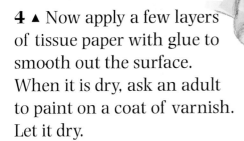

4 ▲ Now apply a few layers of tissue paper with glue to smooth out the surface. When it is dry, ask an adult to paint on a coat of varnish. Let it dry.

SWEET SURPRISE!

This cake looks just like a regular cake—until you cut the first slice! Using cake mix, and making your own fudge icing, prepare to give your family a real surprise . . . .

You will need

1 box cake mix
3½ cups of sugar
2 cups of milk
1 stick of butter, plus extra for greasing the pans
1 medium bar of plain chocolate
2 cake pans, M & Ms, chocolate coins

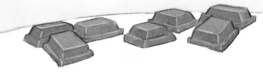

1 First, ask an adult to preheat the oven to 350°F.

2 Grease two cake pans with a little butter. Now make your cake mix, following the instructions on the box, and fill the pans.

To make your fudge icing . . .

3 Ask an adult to help you dissolve the sugar into the milk over medium heat. Bring to a boil, then simmer for two minutes.

4 With an adult, remove the pan from the heat and stir in the chocolate pieces and the butter. Stir over low heat until the chocolate melts. Pour it into a bowl and let it cool.

5 Ask an adult to place the cake pans in the oven. Following the instructions on the box, remove the pans when the cake is done. Turn the cake halves onto a rack to cool.

6 When the cake is cool, cut a circle from inside each half, without cutting through the base. Spread fudge icing around the rims of both halves.

7 Pile chocolate coins into the middle of one half and put the other half on top to make a lid.

8 Cover the whole cake with the rest of the icing. Decorate with M & Ms, slice, and serve. . .surprise!

LIPSMACKIN' LATKES

One of the customs during Hanukkah is to eat fried food. The most traditional of all the fried foods are latkes—potato pancakes. Try these simple recipes for sweet and savory latkes!

You will need

3 medium sized potatoes
1 small onion
2 tablespoons flour
2 eggs (beaten)
$\frac{1}{2}$ teaspoon salt
vegetable oil for frying
a colander, a grater,
a strainer
paper towels
deep skillet

1 Ask an adult to preheat the oven to 200°F.

2 Peel and grate the potatoes into a colander, then leave to drain in the sink. Grate the onion and drain the juice through a strainer.

3 ▶ Mix the potatoes and onion together in a bowl. Stir in the flour, eggs, and salt. Now line a colander with paper towels.

4 ▶ Ask an adult to heat enough oil to fry in a deep skillet. When the oil sizzles, drop in tablespoons of the mixture—spaced apart. Flatten with the back of a spoon. Fry each side until golden brown.

5 ▶ Using a spatula, put the latkes in the lined colander so that the paper can soak up extra oil. Then transfer them to an ovenproof dish and into the oven to keep warm while you make the next batch!

6 ▶ Try switching one potato in the recipe with a small grated zucchini, beet, or carrot to make green, purple, or orange latkes!

BE SURE YOU DON'T BURN YOUR TONGUE!

SWEET CHEESE LATKES

Cheese is a traditional food at this time, so let's cook up some cheesy latkes . . . .

1 Beat the cheese, eggs, flour, butter, sugar, and vanilla flavoring together until smooth and creamy.

2 Lightly grease a large skillet with oil. Put in two tablespoons of the mixture. With an adult, fry the latkes on medium heat until both sides are golden brown. Serve with jelly, ice cream, or applesauce. . .yummy!

You will need

1 cup of ricotta
or cottage cheese
2 large eggs
2 tablespoons flour
1 stick butter
1 tablespoon sugar
1teaspoon vanilla
flavoring
vegetable oil for frying

COOL COOKIES

After you've made your own cookies, how about making icing for them too! Now you can decorate anything—even turn a plain doughnut into a work of art! First, let's make the cookies . . . .

ALMOND COOKIES

You will need

1½ cups of flour
pinch of salt
1¼ sticks of unsalted butter (cut into cubes), plus a little extra for greasing the cookie sheets
cookie cutters or a blunt knife
⅔ cup of sugar
½ cup of ground almonds
one egg, beaten
1 teaspoon almond flavoring
rolling pin

Ask an adult to preheat the oven to 350°F.

1 Sift flour and salt into a bowl. Rub in the butter with your fingers to make fine crumbs.

2 Add the sugar, ground almonds, egg, and almond flavoring. Mix into a ball of dough.

3 On a floured surface, knead the dough gently into a smoother ball. Place it in a plastic bag and refrigerate for 30 minutes.

4 Grease two cookie sheets. On a floured surface roll the chilled dough out to ¼ inch thick.

5 Using cookie cutters or a blunt knife, cut shapes or letters from the dough.

6 Prick the shapes with a fork. Put them on the cookie sheets, and ask an adult to place them in the oven for 12—15 minutes, then remove them. Leave to cool for five minutes, then put them on a wire rack to cool completely.

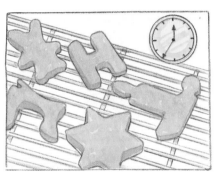

For instant iced treats, take your cookies, a box of plain doughnuts, a cup of sifted confectioners' sugar, colored sprinkles, and make some. . .

ENTICING ICING

Put the sugar into a bowl. Gradually add drops of hot water. Stir until the mixture is smooth and thick enough to coat the back of the spoon. Spread evenly onto your cookies and doughnuts, throw on colored sprinkles, leave to set. . .and serve!

EXCELLENT OILS

Turn olive oil into tasty flavored herbal oil that the whole family will enjoy. . . .

HERBAL OIL

You will need

olive oil, peppercorns, garlic, herbs (bay leaves, basil, sage, tarragon, rosemary, or oregano), old salad dressing bottles or jars with lids or corks, rubber gloves, sticky labels, felt-tip pens

1 Thoroughly wash and dry the old bottles or jars.

2 Choose which herb you want to use—try individual herbs, or combine them with garlic and peppercorns.

3 Wearing rubber gloves, push the flavorings into the bottle and fill it up with olive oil. Replace the lid or cork tightly.

4 Wipe any spilled oil off the bottle and dry it. Label the oil with the ingredients you've used.

SWEET SCENTED OIL

These scented herbal oils are *not* for cooking or swallowing—you put them in the bathtub! Different oils are good for different reasons—rosemary can help wake you up if you're feeling tired, while geranium and lavender are cooling and calming.

You will need

almond oil, a selection of oils such as rosemary, lavender, or geranium (ask an adult to buy these), small plastic or glass bottles with lids or corks, labels, a small funnel, felt-tip pens, rubber gloves

1 ▾ Fill the bottles almost to the top with almond oil. Add drops of rosemary, geranium, or lavender oil.

2 ▾ Put the top on the bottle, tighten, and shake it to mix the oils together.

3 Label the bottle with the name of your oil and what it does. Decorate the label using felt-tip pens and tie a colored ribbon around the lid.

YOUR SCENTED LAMP

If you want to fill a room with the aroma of your scented oils (see page 89), this lamp is easy to make. But remember, *always* ask an adult to light your lamp, and *never* touch it once it is lit.

1 ▾ Split the clay into two balls, each measuring three inches around. Then roll out the balls into two flat circles, each measuring five inches across.

(see page 89)

You will need

DAS clay, strong glue, a rolling pin, two empty yogurt cartons, a small blunt knife, paint, Vaseline, varnish, a small candle, rosemary, lavender, or geranium oil.

2 ▾ Cut one yogurt carton in half. Cover the outside of the bottom half with a coat of Vaseline.

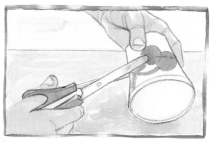 

3 ▾ Cover the outside of the other, whole, carton with Vaseline. Press one clay circle around the sides only. Trim off any extra clay.

5 Cut an arch out of the clay on the larger carton with your knife. Let both cartons dry.

4 ▸ Press the other clay circle over the sides and base of the half carton. Trim the edges with a blunt knife.

6 Remove the cartons. Paint the molds on the outsides only. When dry, put the larger mold on an old saucer. Rest the clay top, safely, on the base.

7 ▼ Put a few drops of one of your scented oils into the top with a tablespoon of water.

8 Place your lamp away from anything that might catch fire. Put a small candle in the base, and ask an adult to light it. The room will be filled with the sweet scent of your oil.

A PERFECT POUCH

This elegant pouch is perfect for keeping loose change in.

You will need
velvet fabric (6in. x 16in.)
iron-on interfacing (6in. x 16in.)
craft paper, pencil,
ruler, scissors, pins,
needle, cotton thread
(same color as velvet)
ten inches of gold cord
small safety pin
gold embroidery thread

1 Ask an adult to iron the interfacing onto the wrong side of the velvet.

2 ► Copy this shape onto paper and cut it out.

6 in.

3 in.

3 ► With an adult's help, pin the pattern to the velvet and cut around it. Repeat four times to make four sides for the pouch.

4 ◄ Pin the edges together with the right sides facing each other. Sew, leaving a $^1/_2$-inch wide seam.

5 ► Turn over the top $^1/_2$ inch, and then again $^3/_4$ inch to make a casing for the cord. Pin and sew the casing in place. Leave a $^1/_2$-inch gap to thread the cord through.

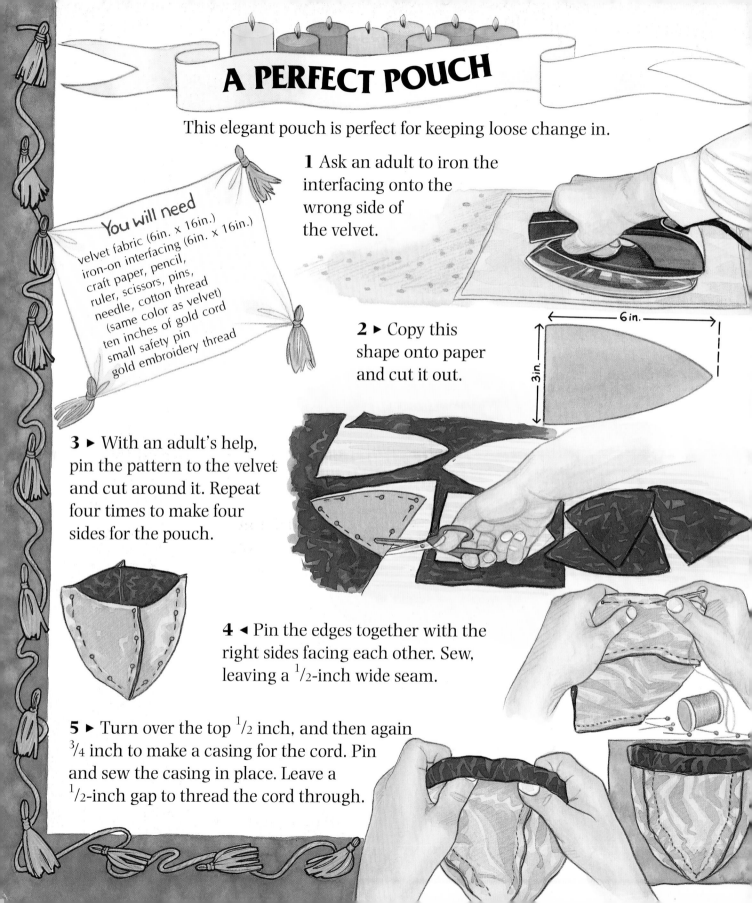

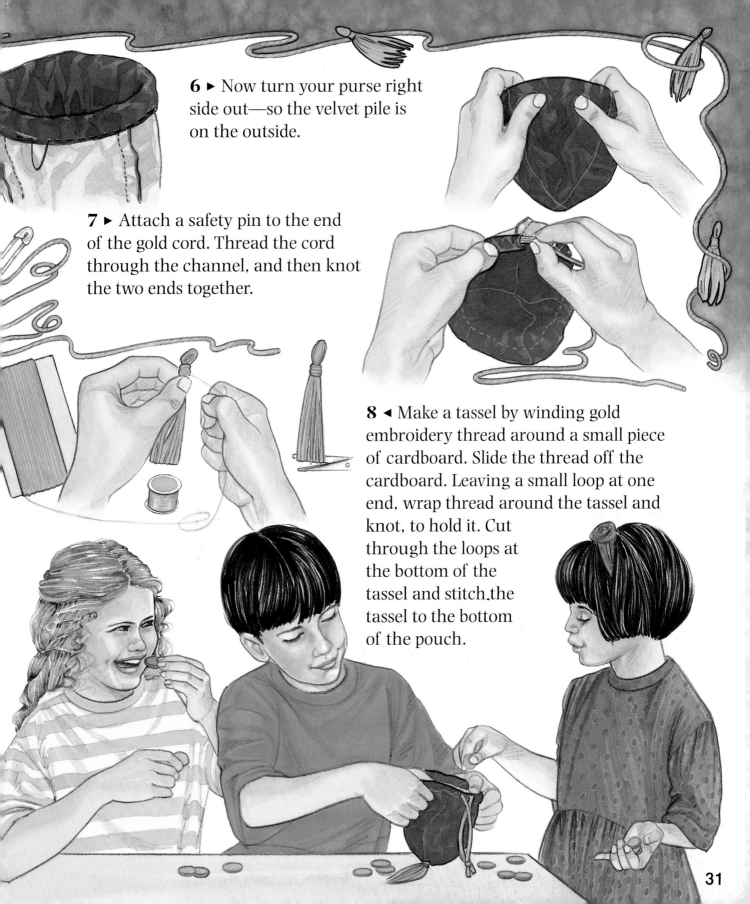

6 ▶ Now turn your purse right side out—so the velvet pile is on the outside.

7 ▶ Attach a safety pin to the end of the gold cord. Thread the cord through the channel, and then knot the two ends together.

8 ◀ Make a tassel by winding gold embroidery thread around a small piece of cardboard. Slide the thread off the cardboard. Leaving a small loop at one end, wrap thread around the tassel and knot, to hold it. Cut through the loops at the bottom of the tassel and stitch.the tassel to the bottom of the pouch.

YOUR HEBREW LETTERS

The Hebrew letters you have seen inside this book are *Nun, Gimel, Heh,* and *Shin,* and they have a special meaning at Hanukkah. The letters stand for the words *Nes gadol hayah sham,* which means "a great miracle happened there." In Israel they say *Nes gadol hayah po*— "a great miracle happened *here.*" The miracle is of the Hanukkah lights burning for eight days and nights. The letters shown here should always be read from right to left and should always go on the dreidel in the order shown below. . . .

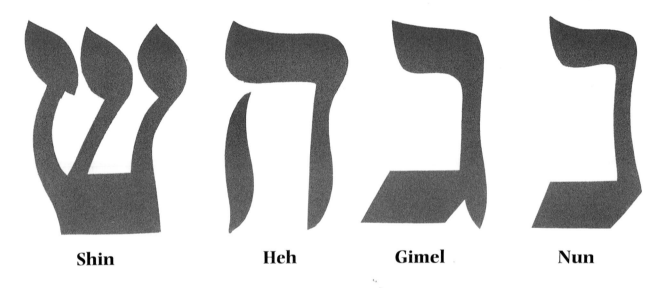

Shin   **Heh**   **Gimel**   **Nun**

Have fun making all the things inside this book, and have the happiest of Hanukkahs!